CHRISTMAS *Ukulele Solos*

Arranged by Tom Huizinga

ISBN 978-1-4803-4557-7

HAL•LEONARD®
CORPORATION

7777 W. BLUEMOUND RD. P.O. BOX 13819 MILWAUKEE, WI 53213

Visit Hal Leonard Online at
www.halleonard.com

UKULELE NOTATION LEGEND

THE MUSICAL STAFF shows pitches and rhythms and is divided by bar lines into measures. Pitches are named after the first seven letters of the alphabet.

TABLATURE graphically represents the ukulele fingerboard. Each horizontal line represents a a string, and each number represents a fret.

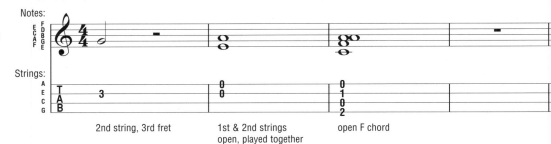

2nd string, 3rd fret   1st & 2nd strings open, played together   open F chord

HALF-STEP BEND: Strike the note and bend up 1/2 step.

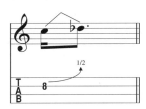

WHOLE-STEP BEND: Strike the note and bend up one step.

GRACE NOTE BEND: Strike the note and immediately bend up as indicated.

SLIGHT (MICROTONE) BEND: Strike the note and bend up 1/4 step.

BEND AND RELEASE: Strike the note and bend up as indicated, then release back to the original note. Only the first note is struck.

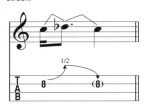

PRE-BEND: Bend the note as indicated, then strike it.

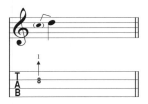

VIBRATO: The string is vibrated by rapidly bending and releasing the note with the fretting hand.

HAMMER-ON: Strike the first (lower) note with one finger, then sound the higher note (on the same string) with another finger by fretting it without picking.

PULL-OFF: Place both fingers on the notes to be sounded. Strike the first note and without picking, pull the finger off to sound the second (lower) note.

LEGATO SLIDE: Strike the first note and then slide the same fret-hand finger up or down to the second note. The second note is not struck.

SHIFT SLIDE: Same as legato slide, except the second note is struck.

TRILL: Very rapidly alternate between the notes indicated by continuously hammering on and pulling off.

TREMOLO PICKING: The note is picked as rapidly and continuously as possible.

Additional Musical Definitions

 (accent) • Accentuate note (play it louder)

 (staccato) • Play the note short

D.S. al Coda • Go back to the sign (𝄋), then play until the measure marked "***To Coda***," then skip to the section labelled "**Coda**."

D.C. al Fine • Go back to the beginning of the song and play until the measure marked "***Fine***" (end).

N.C. • No chord.

 • Repeat measures between signs.

 • When a repeated section has different endings, play the first ending only the first time and the second ending only the second time.

NOTE: Tablature numbers in parentheses mean:

1. The note is being sustained over a system (note in standard notation is tied), or

2. The note is sustained, but a new articulation (such as a hammer-on, pull-off, slide or vibrato) begins, or

3. The note is a barely audible "ghost" note (note in standard notation is also in parentheses).

Contents

All I Want for Christmas
Is My Two Front Teeth

Words and Music by Don Gardner

Low G tuning:
(low to high) G-C-E-A

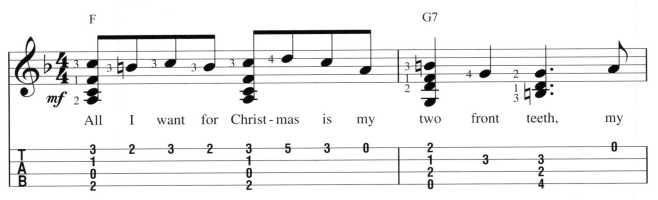

Chorus
Moderately

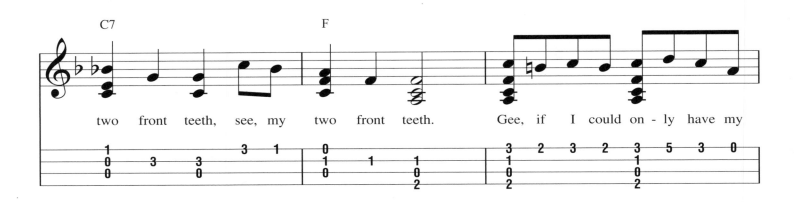

All I want for Christ-mas is my two front teeth, my

two front teeth, see, my two front teeth. Gee, if I could on-ly have my

two front teeth, then I could wish you, "Mer-ry Christ-mas!" 1. It

Verse

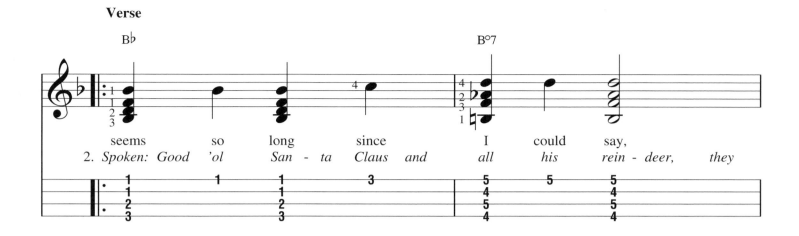

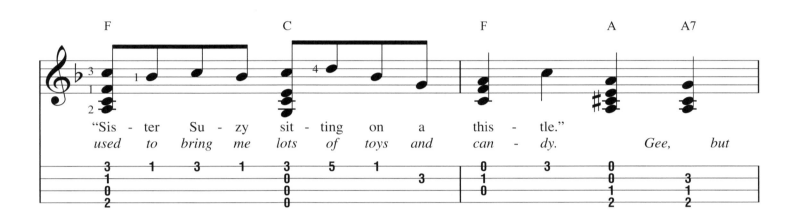

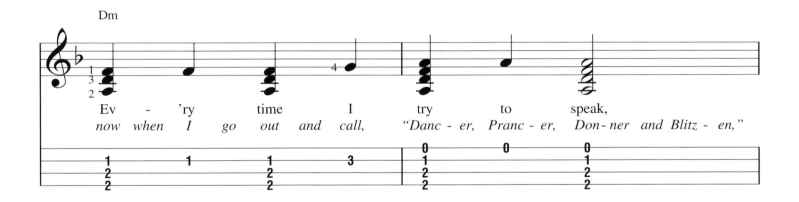

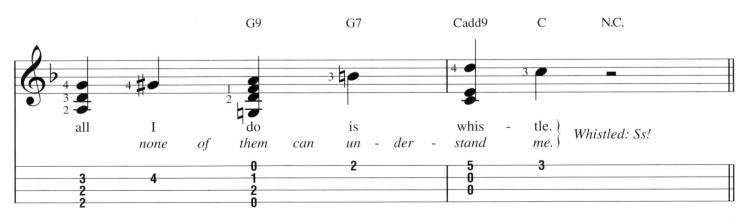

Outro-Chorus

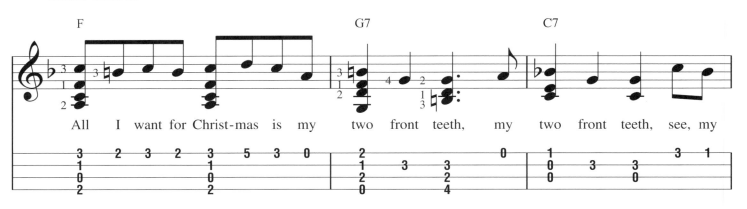

All I want for Christ-mas is my two front teeth, my two front teeth, see, my

two front teeth. Gee, if I could on - ly have my two front teeth, then
All I want for Christ-mas is my two front teeth, so

I could wish you, "Mer - ry Christ - mas!" Christ - mas!" Christ -
I can wish you, "Mer - ry

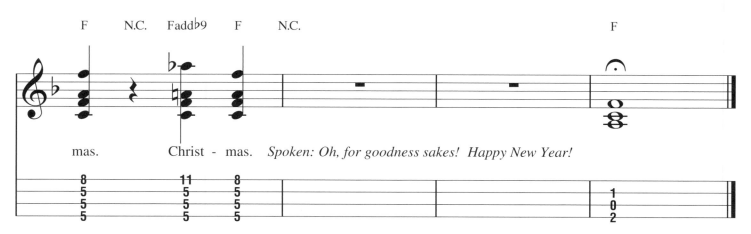

mas. Christ - mas. *Spoken: Oh, for goodness sakes! Happy New Year!*

Blue Christmas

Words and Music by Billy Hayes and Jay Johnson

Low G tuning:
(low to high) G-C-E-A

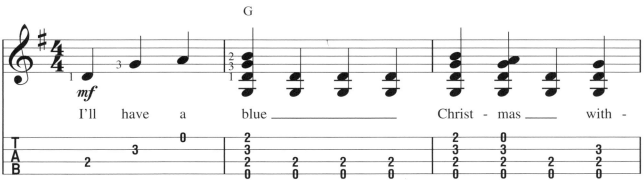

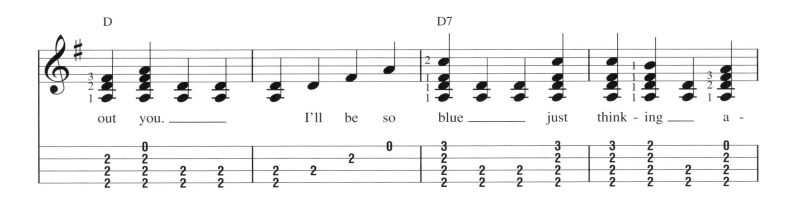

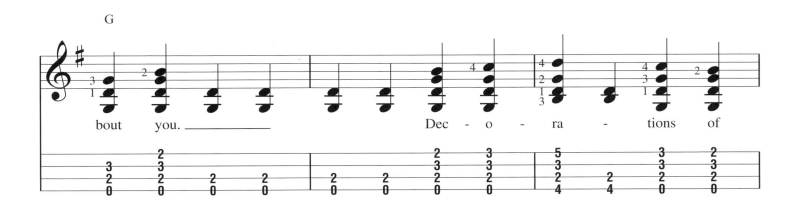

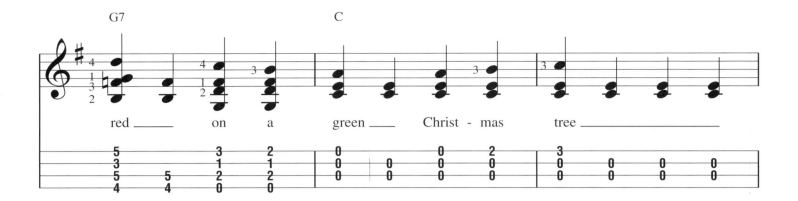

red _____ on a green _____ Christ - mas tree _____

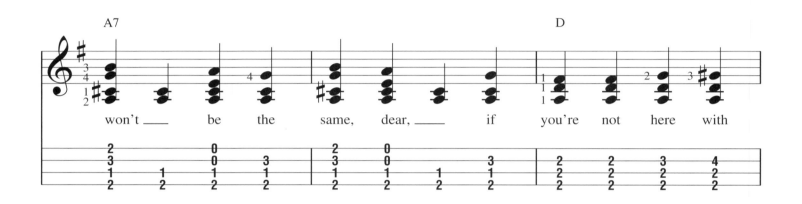

won't _____ be the same, dear, _____ if you're not here with

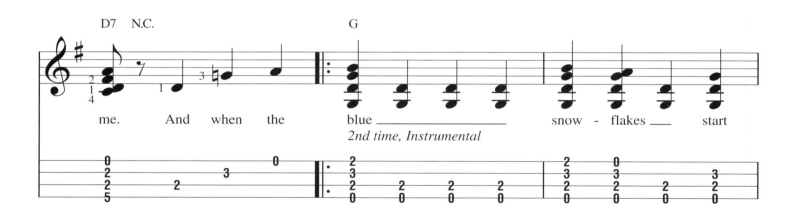

me. And when the blue _____ snow - flakes _____ start

2nd time, Instrumental

fall - in', _____ that's when those blue _____

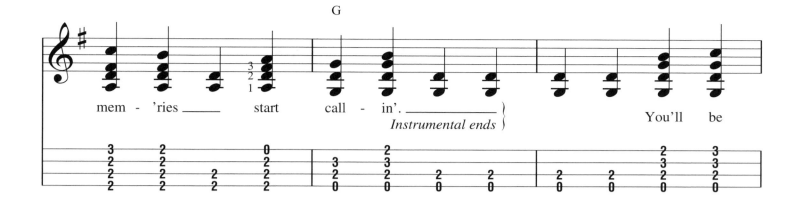

mem - 'ries _____ start call - in'. _____
Instrumental ends
You'll be

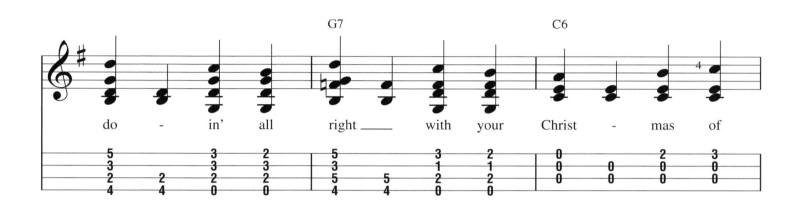

do - in' all right _____ with your Christ - mas of

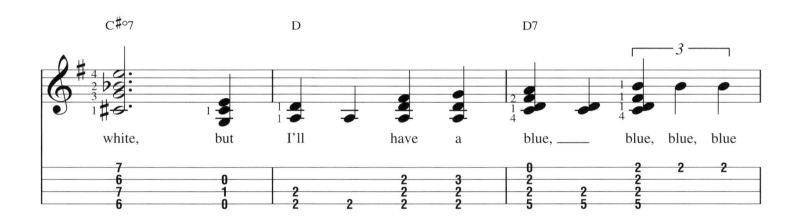

white, but I'll have a blue, _____ blue, blue, blue

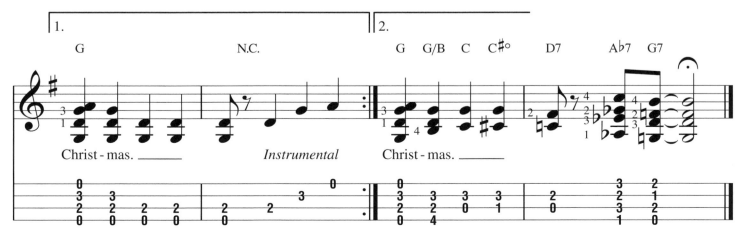

Christ - mas. _____ *Instrumental* Christ - mas. _____

The Christmas Song
(Chestnuts Roasting on an Open Fire)

Music and Lyric by Mel Torme and Robert Wells

Low G tuning:
(low to high) G-C-E-A

Verse
Slow

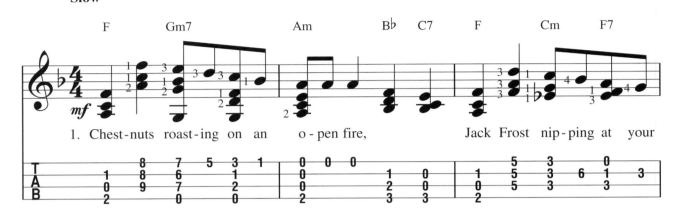

1. Chest-nuts roast-ing on an o-pen fire, Jack Frost nip-ping at your

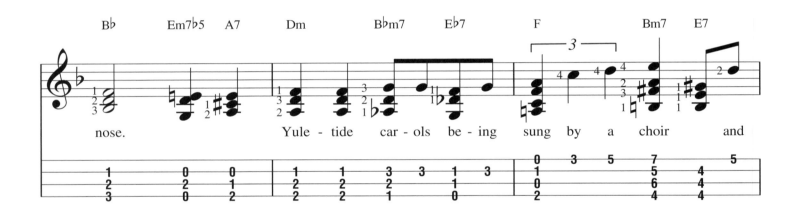

nose. Yule-tide car-ols be-ing sung by a choir and

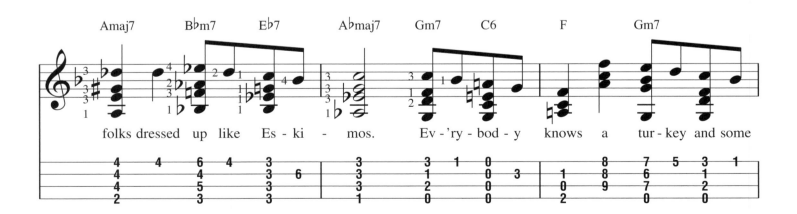

folks dressed up like Es-ki-mos. Ev-'ry-bod-y knows a tur-key and some

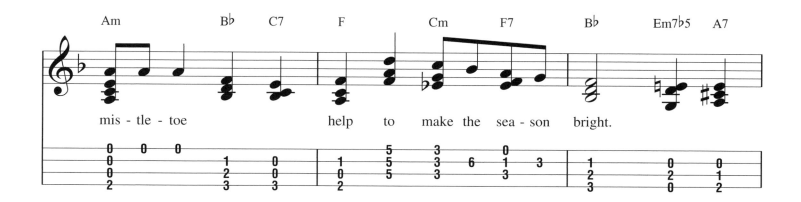

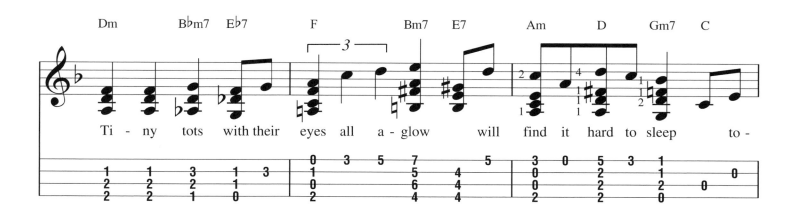

Bridge

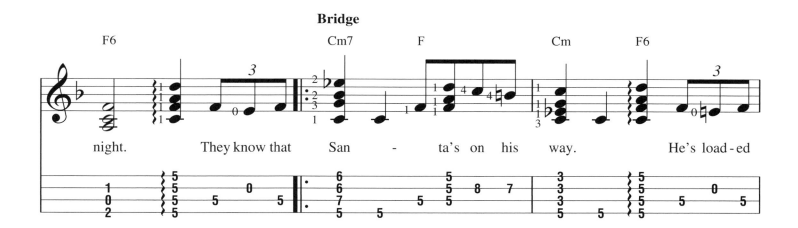

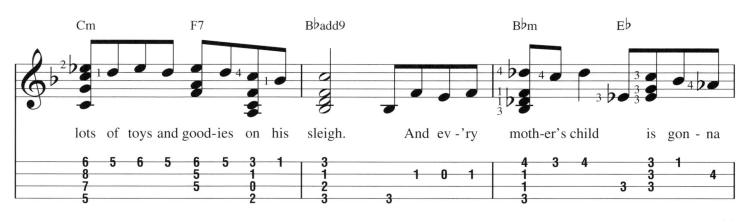

spy   to see if   rein-deer real - ly know how to   fly.   2., 3. And

Verse

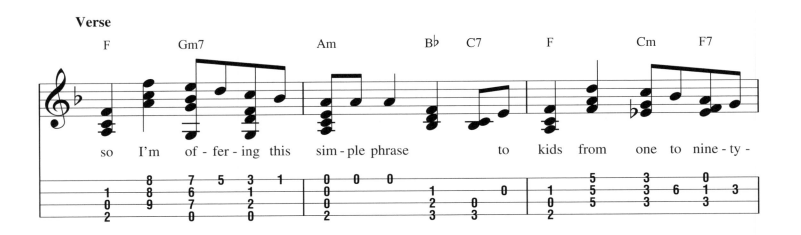

so   I'm   of - fer - ing this   sim - ple phrase   to   kids from   one to nine - ty -

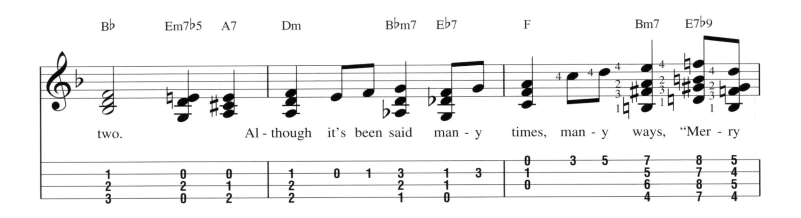

two.   Al - though   it's been said   man - y   times, man - y   ways, "Mer - ry

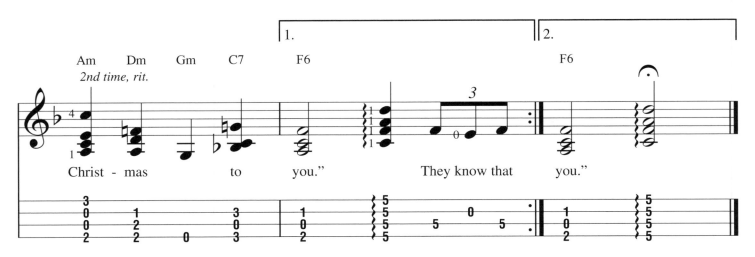

Christ - mas   to   you."   They know that   you."

The Christmas Waltz

Words by Sammy Cahn
Music by Jule Styne

Low G tuning:
(low to high) G-C-E-A

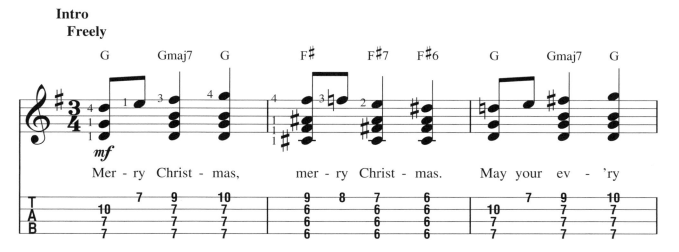

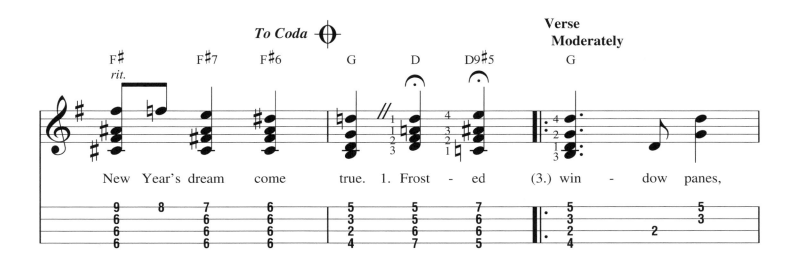

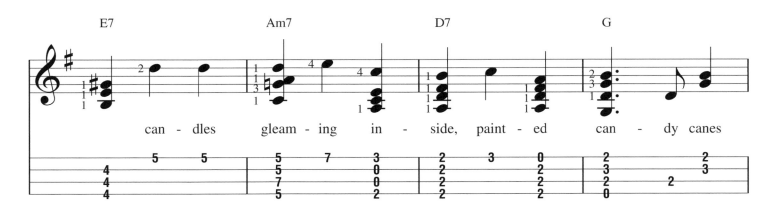

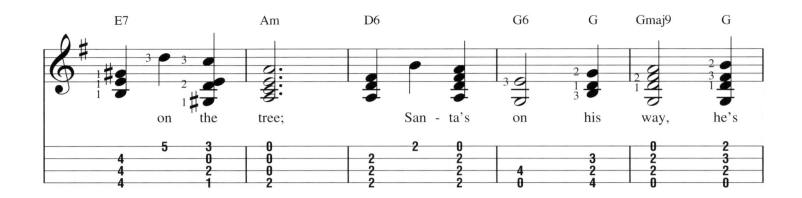

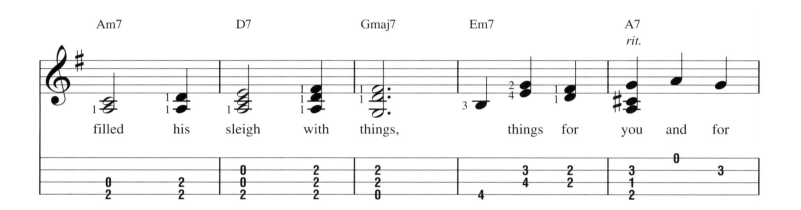

Verse
A tempo

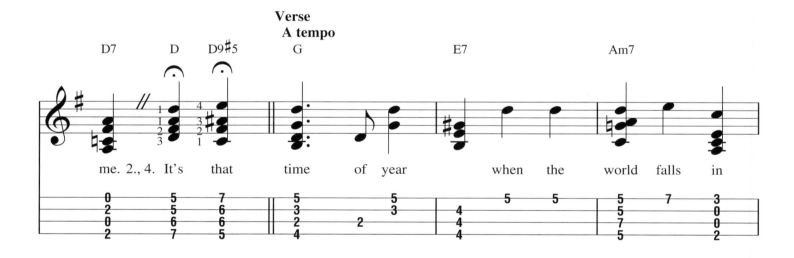

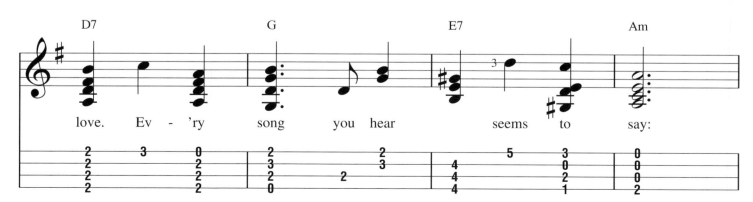

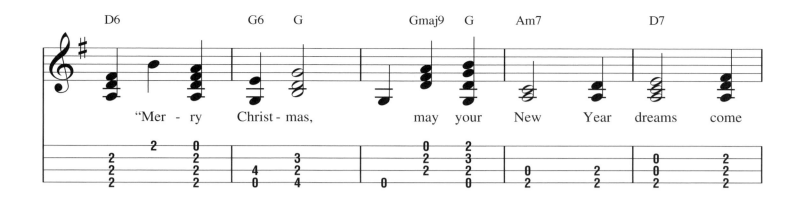

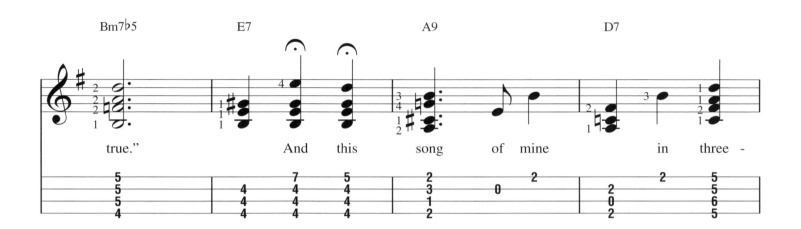

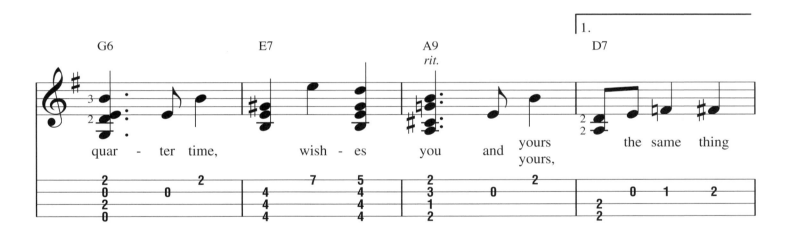

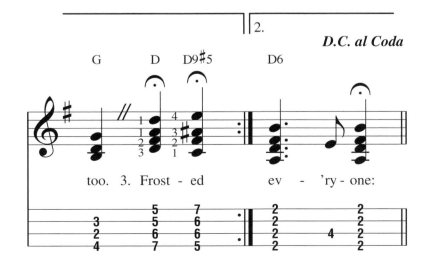

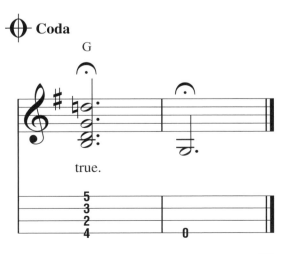

Christmas Time Is Here

from A CHARLIE BROWN CHRISTMAS

Words by Lee Mendelson
Music by Vince Guaraldi

Do You Hear What I Hear

Words and Music by Noel Regney and Gloria Shayne

Additional Lyrics

3. Said the shepherd boy to the mighty king,
   Do you know what I know? (Do you know what I know?)
   In your palace warm, mighty king,
   Do you know what I know? (Do you know what I know?)
   A Child, a Child shivers in the cold,
   Let us bring Him silver and gold,
   Let us bring Him silver and gold.

4. Said the king to the people ev'rywhere,
   Listen to what I say! (Listen to what I say!)
   Pray for peace, people ev'rywhere,
   Listen to what I say! (Listen to what I say!)
   The Child, the Child, sleeping in the night,
   He will bring us goodness and light,
   He will bring us goodness and light.

Feliz Navidad

Music and Lyrics by José Feliciano

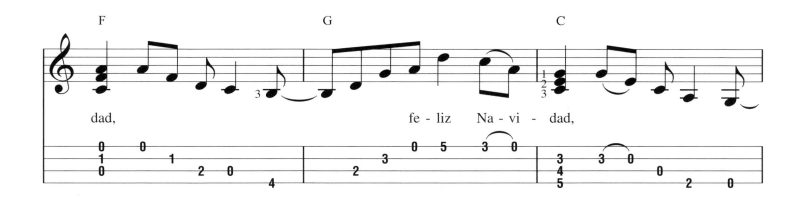

dad,   fe - liz   Na - vi - dad,

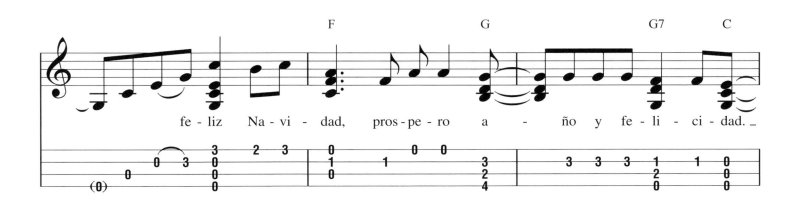

fe - liz   Na - vi - dad,   pros - pe - ro   a - ño y fe - li - ci - dad. _

Verse

1., 2. I want to wish   you   a   mer - ry Christ - mas,

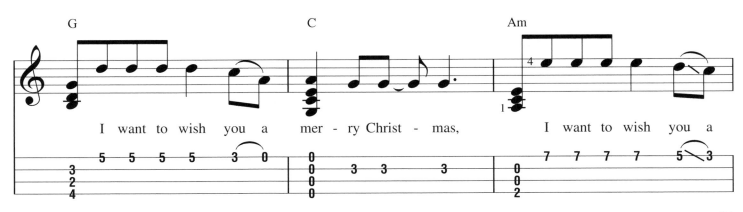

I want to wish   you   a   mer - ry Christ - mas,   I want to wish   you   a

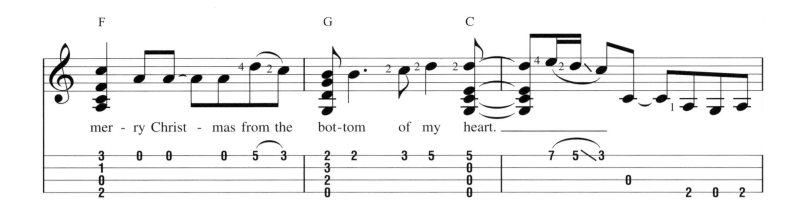

mer - ry Christ - mas from the   bot-tom   of   my   heart. _____

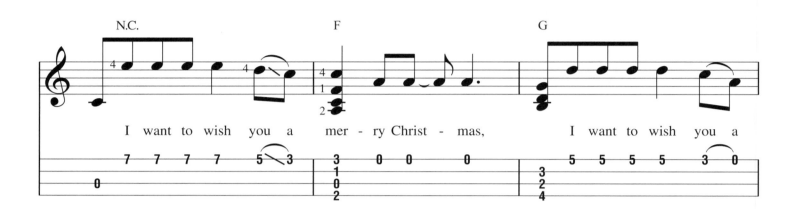

I want to wish   you   a   mer - ry Christ - mas,   I want to wish   you   a

mer - ry Christ - mas,   I want to wish   you   a   mer - ry Christ - mas from the

2nd time, D.S. al Fine

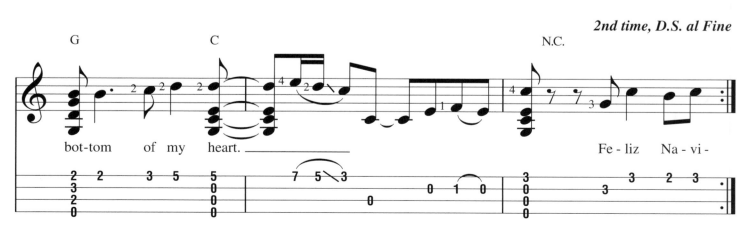

bot-tom   of   my   heart. _____   Fe - liz   Na - vi -

Frosty the Snow Man

Words and Music by Steve Nelson and Jack Rollins

Low G tuning:
(low to high) G-C-E-A

Have Yourself a Merry Little Christmas

Words and Music by Hugh Martin and Ralph Blane

From now on our trou-bles will be miles a - way.

Bridge

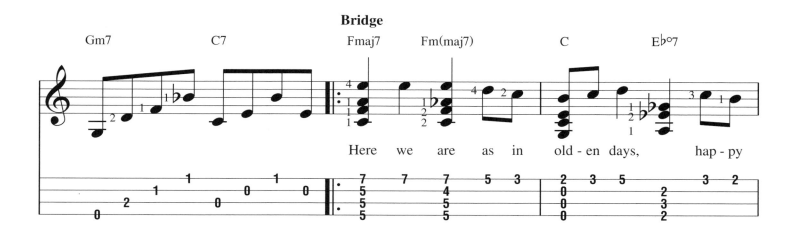

Here we are as in old - en days, hap - py

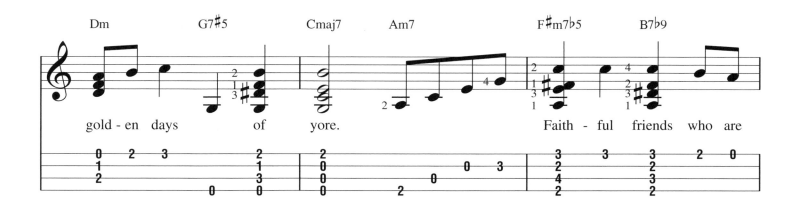

gold - en days of yore. Faith - ful friends who are

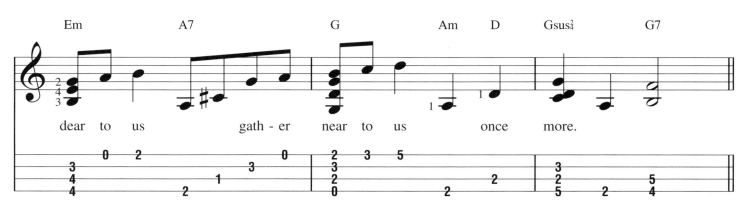

dear to us gath - er near to us once more.

Verse

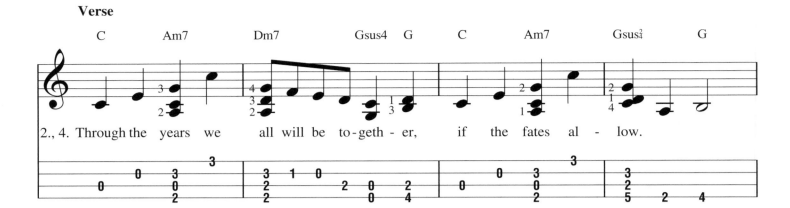

2., 4. Through the years we all will be to-geth - er, if the fates al - low.

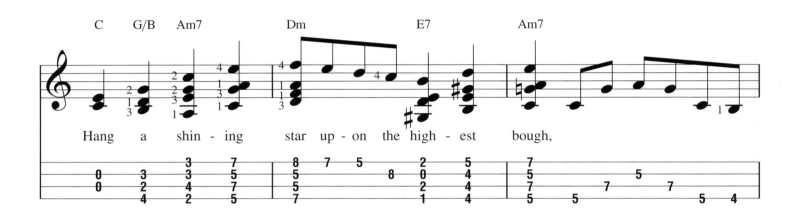

Hang a shin - ing star up - on the high - est bough,

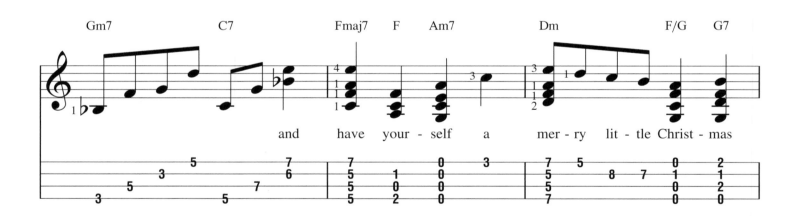

and have your - self a mer - ry lit - tle Christ - mas

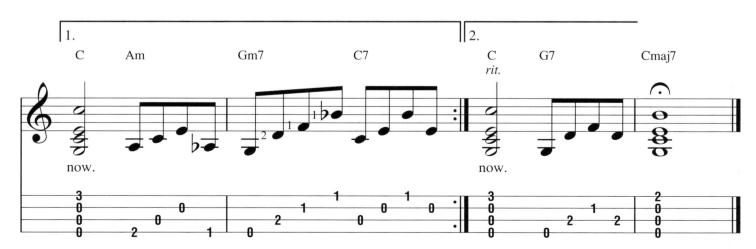

now.

now.

Jingle Bell Rock

Words and Music by Joe Beal and Jim Boothe

(There's No Place Like)
Home for the Holidays

Words and Music by Al Stillman and Robert Allen

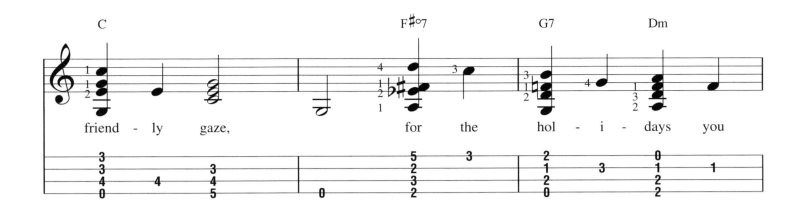

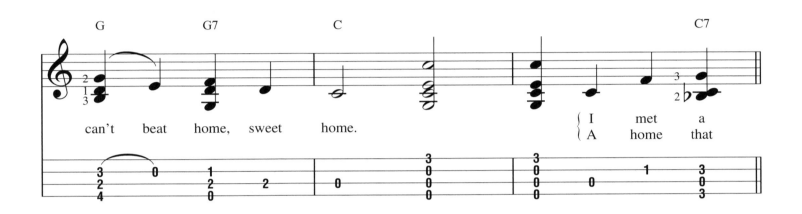

Bridge

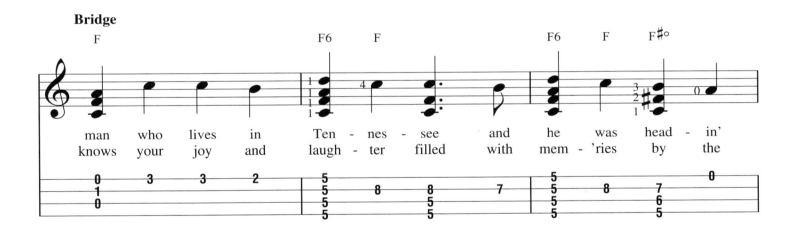

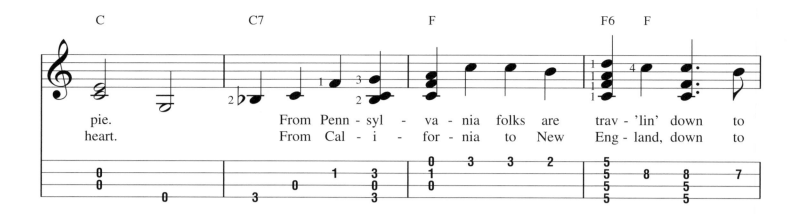

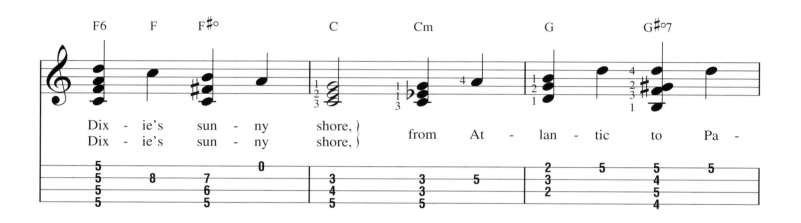

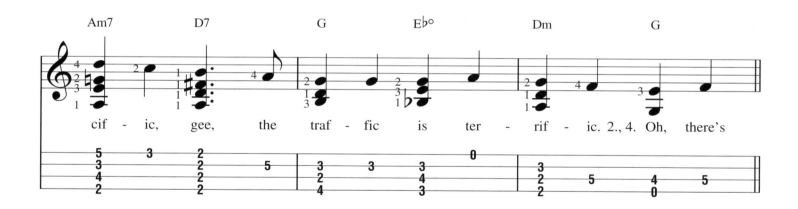

Verse

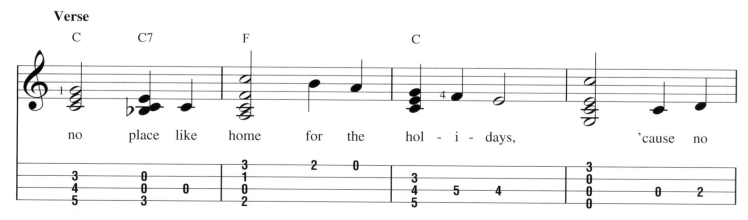

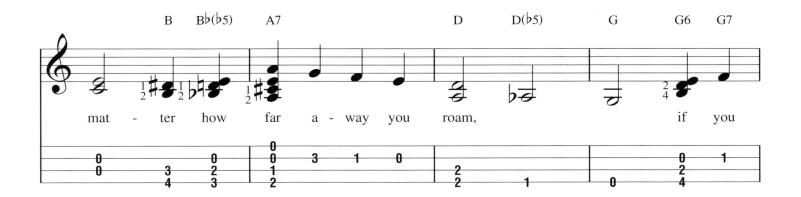

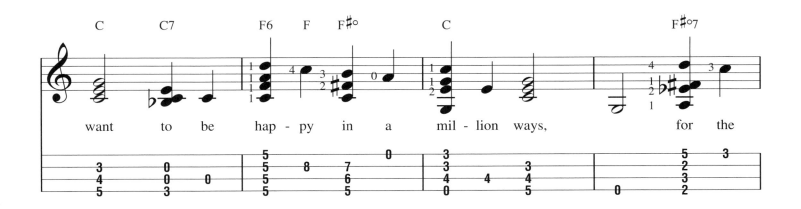

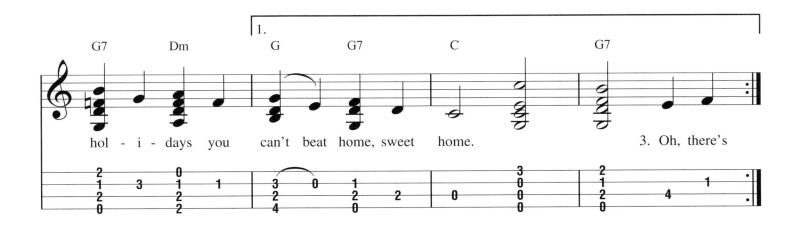

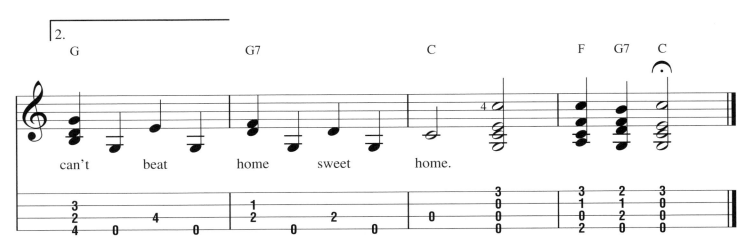

The Little Drummer Boy

Words and Music by Harry Simeone, Henry Onorati and Katherine Davis

Low G tuning:
(low to high) G-C-E-A

Intro
Slow, in 2

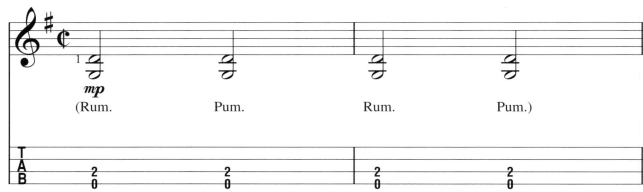

*Chord symbols reflect implied harmony.

Verse

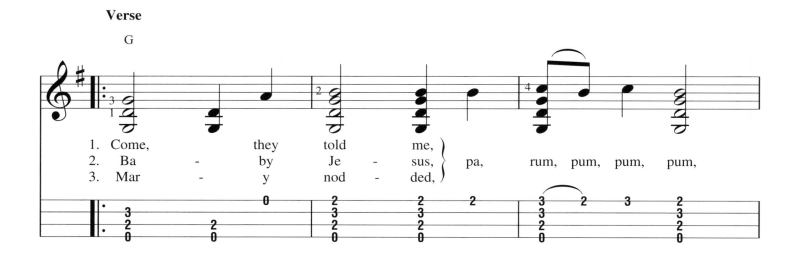

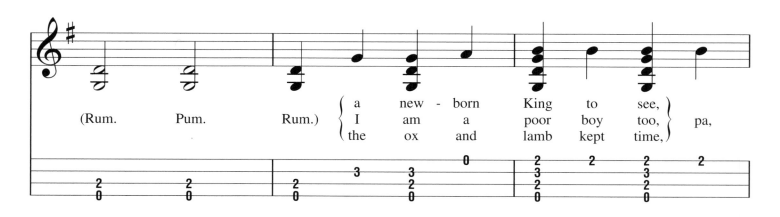

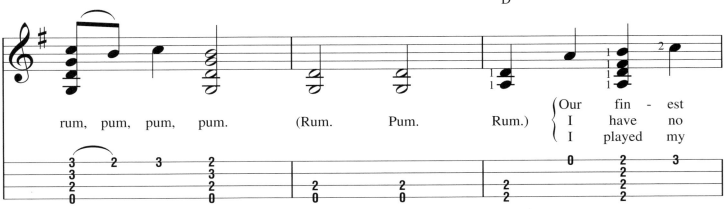

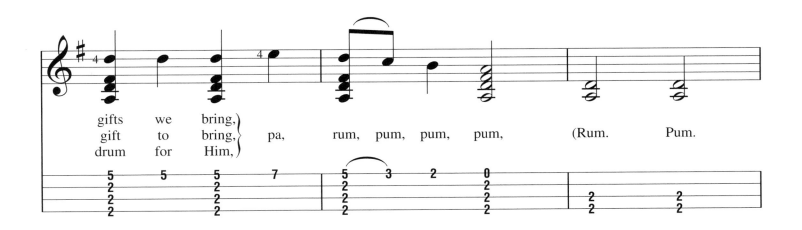

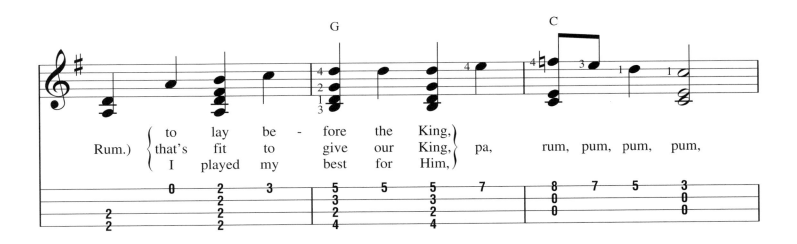

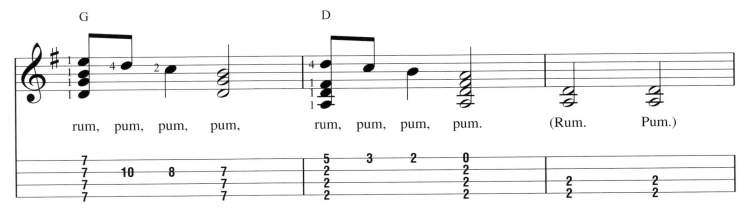

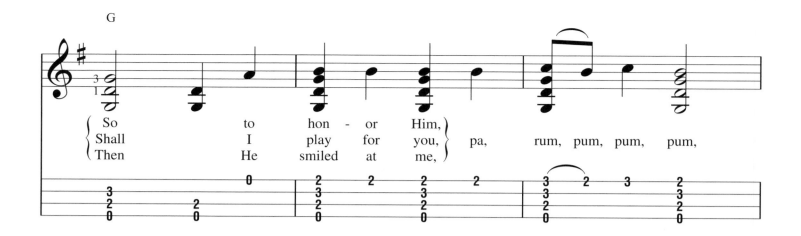

So to hon - or Him,
Shall I play for you, pa, rum, pum, pum, pum,
Then He smiled at me,

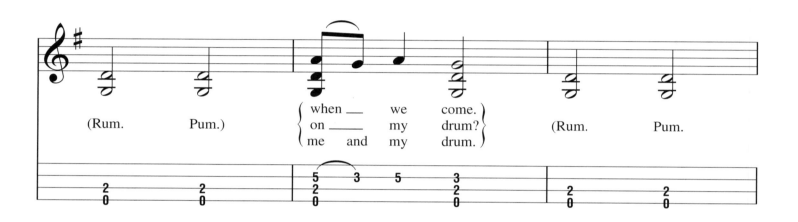

(Rum. Pum.)
when ___ we come.
on ___ my drum? (Rum. Pum.
me and my drum.)

Play 3 times

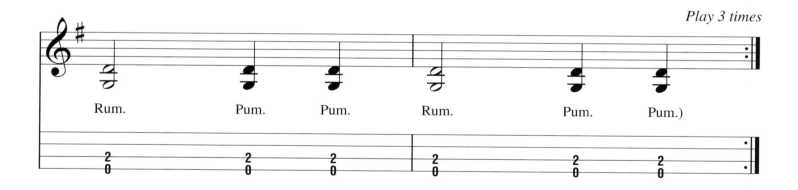

Rum. Pum. Pum. Rum. Pum. Pum.)

Outro

G

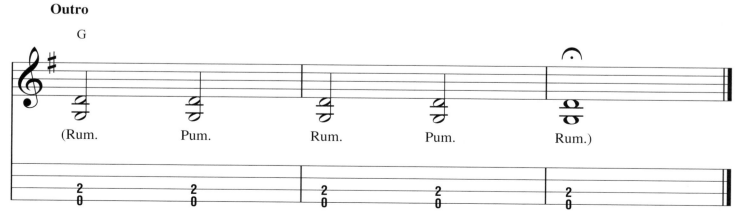

(Rum. Pum. Rum. Pum. Rum.)

Mistletoe and Holly

Words and Music by Frank Sinatra, Dok Stanford and Henry W. Sanicola

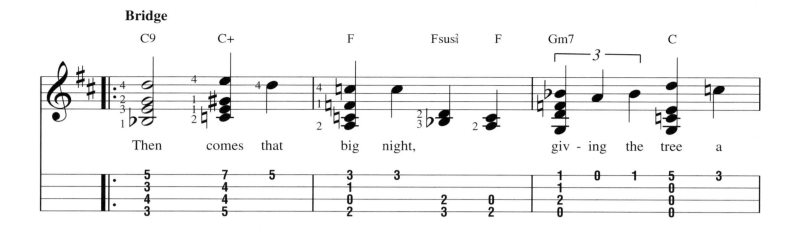

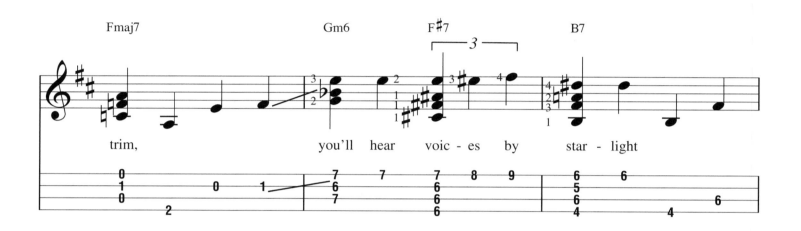

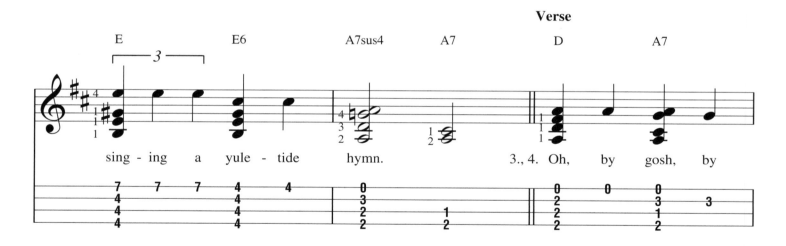

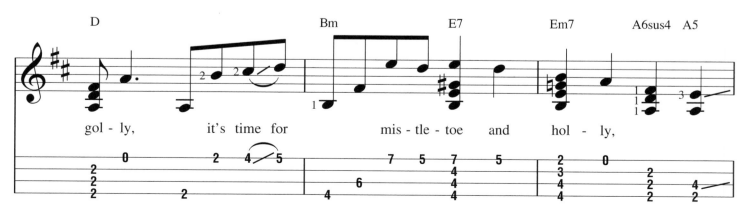

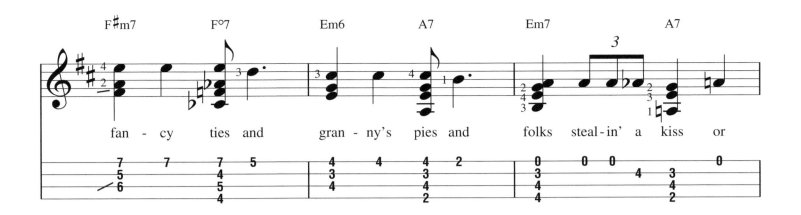

fan - cy   ties   and   gran - ny's   pies   and   folks   steal - in'   a   kiss   or

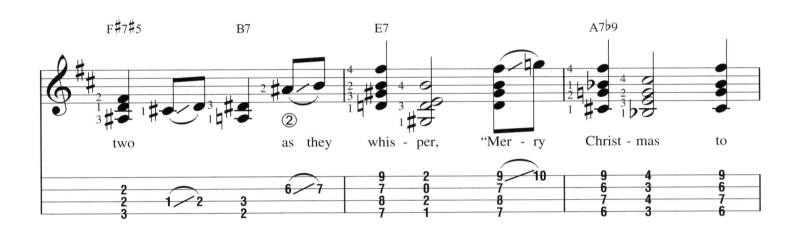

two   as   they   whis - per,   "Mer - ry   Christ - mas   to

you."

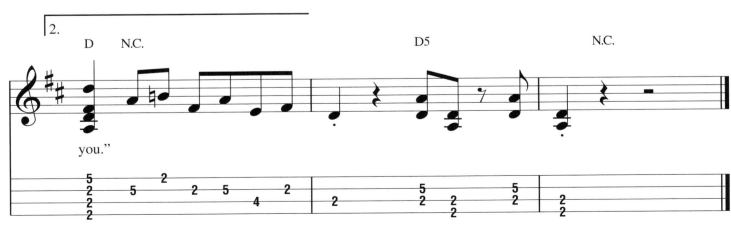

you."

Merry Christmas, Darling

Words and Music by Richard Carpenter and Frank Pooler

Low G tuning:
(low to high) G-C-E-A

Intro

Moderately slow

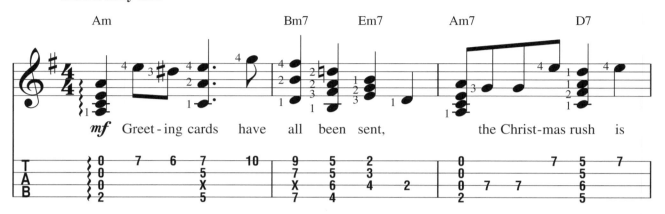

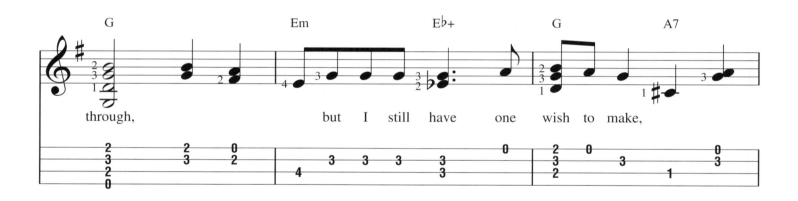

Verse

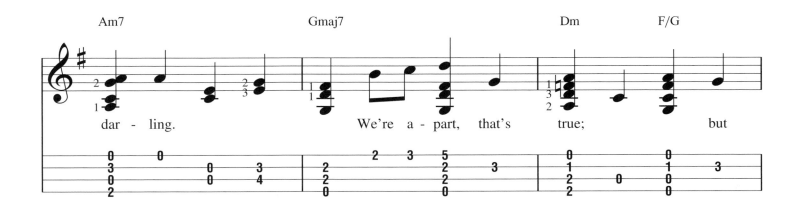

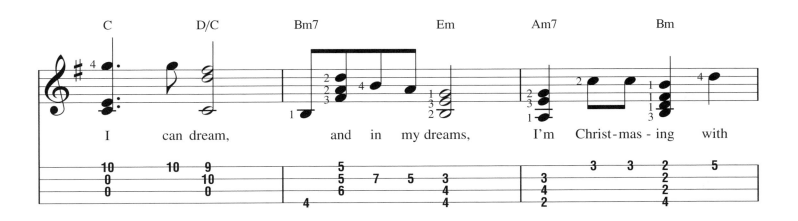

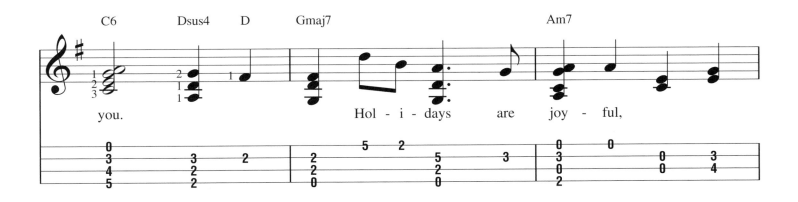

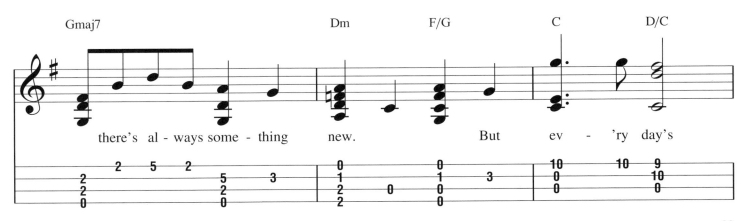

a hol - i - day   when I'm near   to   you.   The __

Bridge

lights   on   my   tree   I   wish   you could see,   I   wish   it   ev - 'ry
2nd time, Instrumental

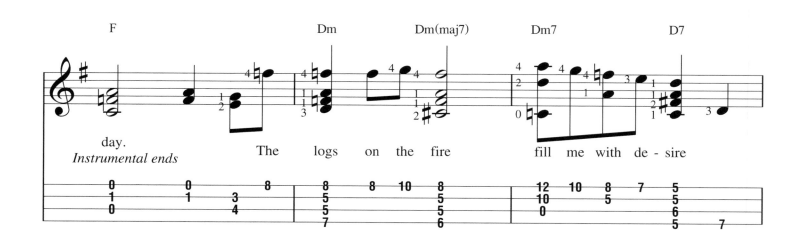

day.   The   logs   on   the   fire   fill   me   with   de - sire
Instrumental ends

Verse

to   see   you   and   to __   say   2., 3. that   I   wish   you mer - ry

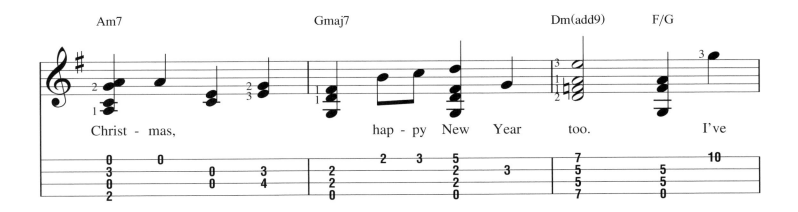

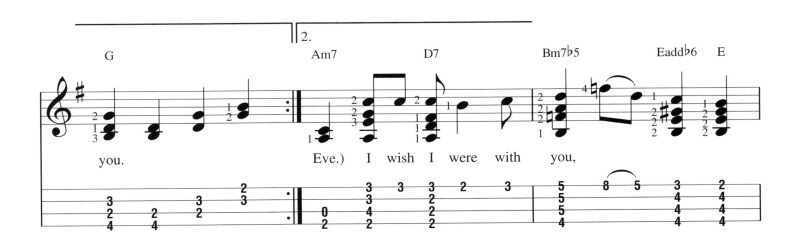

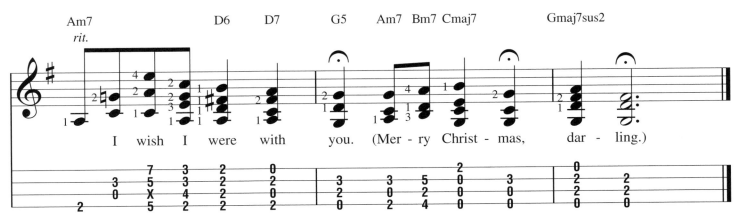

Rudolph the Red-Nosed Reindeer

Music and Lyrics by Johnny Marks

Low G tuning:
(low to high) G-C-E-A

Intro
Freely

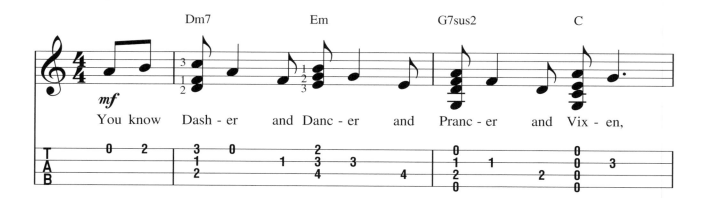

You know Dash - er and Danc - er and Pranc - er and Vix - en,

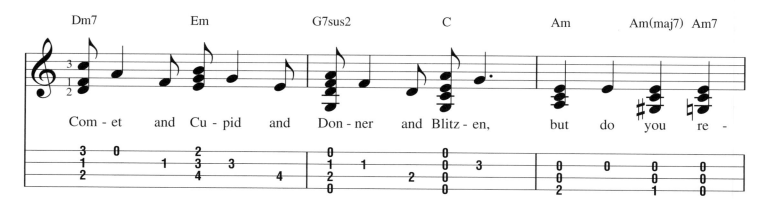

Com - et and Cu - pid and Don - ner and Blitz - en, but do you re -

Moderately

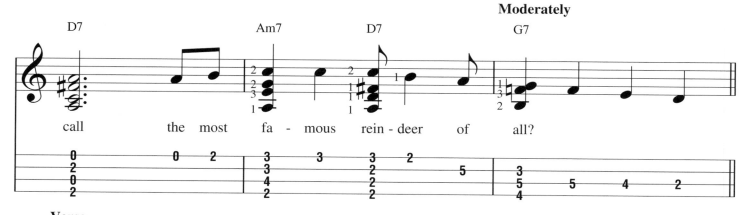

call the most fa - mous rein - deer of all?

Verse

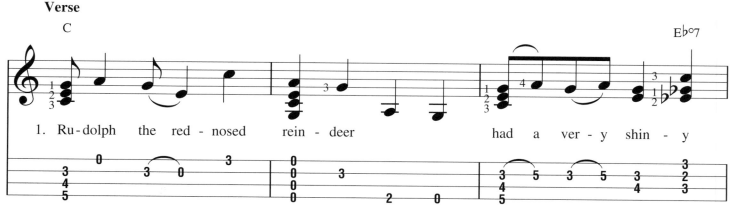

1. Ru - dolph the red - nosed rein - deer had a ver - y shin - y

Silver Bells

from the Paramount Picture THE LEMON DROP KID
Words and Music by Jay Livingston and Ray Evans

Low G tuning:
(low to high) G-C-E-A

Chorus
Moderately slow

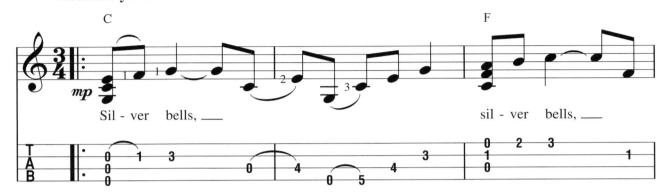

Sil - ver bells, ___ sil - ver bells, ___

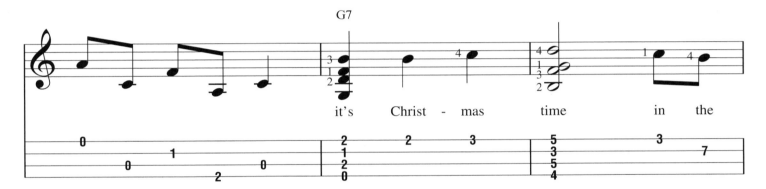

it's Christ - mas time in the

cit - y. Ring - a - ling, _____

To Coda ⊕

hear them ring, _____

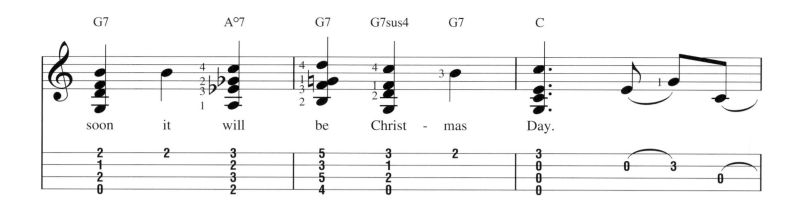

soon it will be Christ - mas Day.

Verse

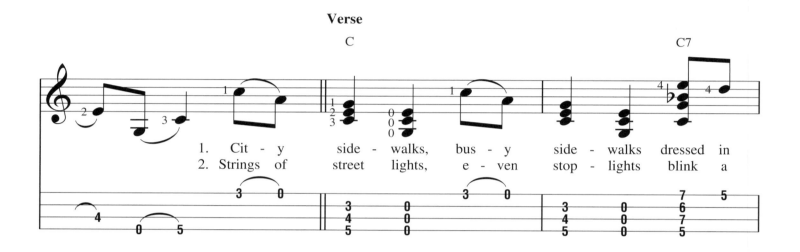

1. Cit - y side - walks, bus - y side - walks dressed in
2. Strings of street lights, e - ven stop - lights blink a

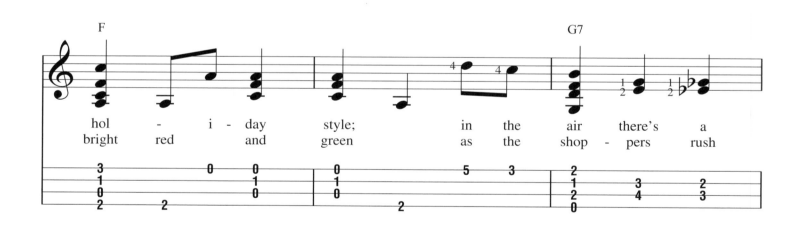

hol - i - day style; in the air there's a
bright red and green as the shop - pers rush

feel - ing of Christ - mas. _____ Chil - dren
home with their treas - ures. _____ Hear the

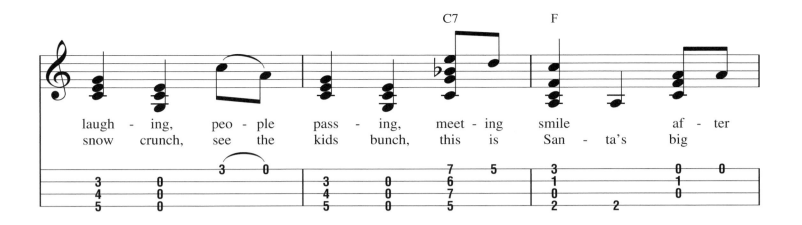

laugh - ing, peo - ple pass - ing, meet - ing smile af - ter
snow crunch, see the kids bunch, this is San - ta's big

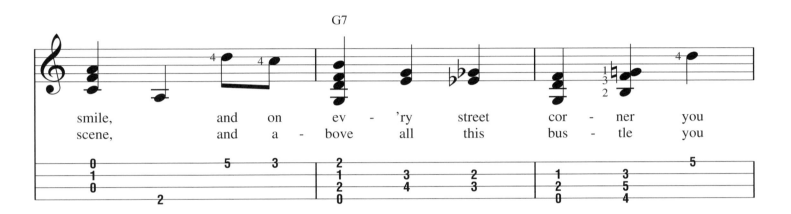

smile, and on ev - 'ry street cor - ner you
scene, and a - bove all this bus - tle you

2nd time, D.C. al Coda   ⊕ **Coda**

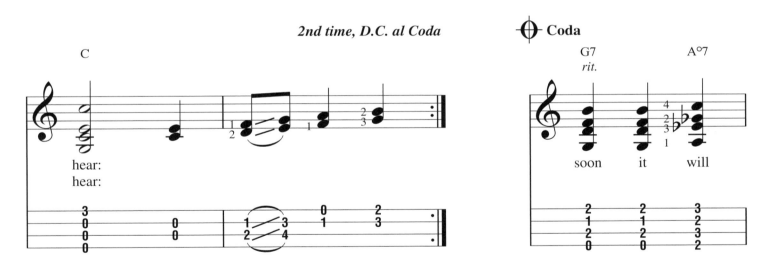

hear:
hear:

soon it will

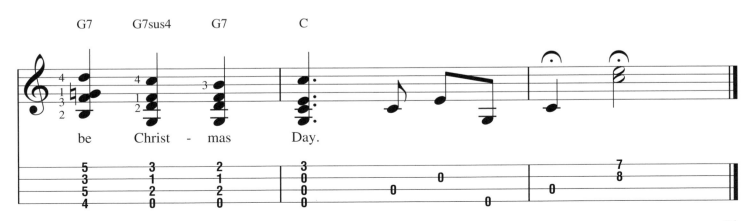

be Christ - mas Day.

Sleigh Ride

Music by Leroy Anderson
Words by Mitchell Parish

Low G tuning:
(low to high) G-C-E-A

Moderately slow, in 2

1. Just hear those (3.) sleigh bells jin-gl-ing, ring, ting, tin-gl-ing too.

Come on, it's love-ly weath-er for a sleigh ride to-geth-er with you.

Out-side the snow is fall-ing and friends are call-ing, "Yoo hoo."

Come on, it's love-ly weath-er for a sleigh ride to-geth-er with you.

Snowfall

Lyrics by Ruth Thornhill
Music by Claude Thornhill

White Christmas

Words and Music by Irving Berlin

Low G tuning:
(low to high) G-C-E-A

Verse
Moderately slow

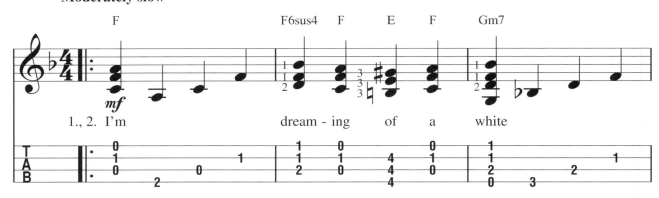

1., 2. I'm dream - ing of a white

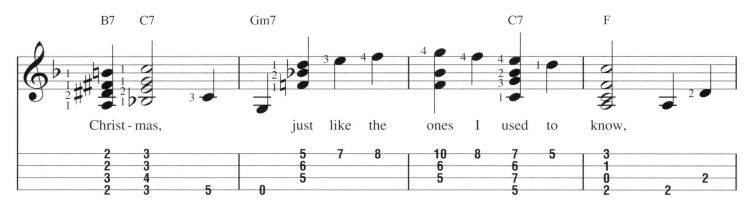

Christ - mas, just like the ones I used to know,

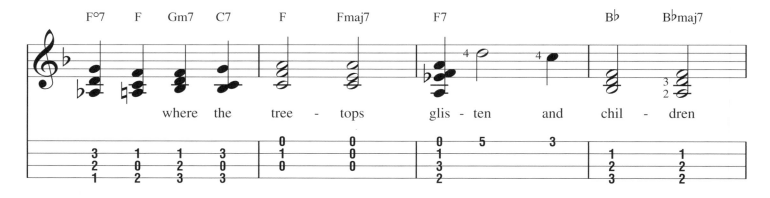

where the tree - tops glis - ten and chil - dren

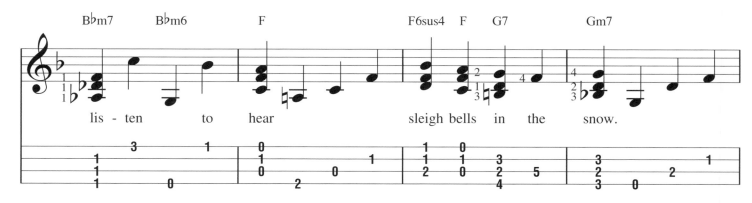

lis - ten to hear sleigh bells in the snow.

Winter Wonderland

Words by Dick Smith
Music by Felix Bernard

Low G tuning:
(low to high) G-C-E-A

HAL·LEONARD UKULELE PLAY-ALONG

Now you can play your favorite songs on your uke with great-sounding backing tracks to help you sound like a bona fide pro!

1. POP HITS
00701451 Book/CD Pack.........................$14.99

2. UKE CLASSICS
00701452 Book/CD Pack.........................$12.99

3. HAWAIIAN FAVORITES
00701453 Book/CD Pack.........................$12.99

4. CHILDREN'S SONGS
00701454 Book/CD Pack.........................$12.99

5. CHRISTMAS SONGS
00701696 Book/CD Pack.........................$12.99

6. LENNON & McCARTNEY
00701723 Book/CD Pack.........................$12.99

7. DISNEY FAVORITES
00701724 Book/CD Pack.........................$12.99

8. CHART HITS
00701745 Book/CD Pack.........................$14.99

9. THE SOUND OF MUSIC
00701784 Book/CD Pack.........................$12.99

10. MOTOWN
00701964 Book/CD Pack.........................$12.99

11. CHRISTMAS STRUMMING
00702458 Book/CD Pack.........................$12.99

12. BLUEGRASS FAVORITES
00702584 Book/CD Pack.........................$12.99

13. UKULELE SONGS
00702599 Book/CD Pack.........................$12.99

14. JOHNNY CASH
00702615 Book/CD Pack.........................$14.99

15. COUNTRY CLASSICS
00702834 Book/CD Pack.........................$12.99

16. STANDARDS
00702835 Book/CD Pack.........................$12.99

17. POP STANDARDS
00702836 Book/CD Pack.........................$12.99

18. IRISH SONGS
00703086 Book/CD Pack.........................$12.99

19. BLUES STANDARDS
00703087 Book/CD Pack.........................$12.99

20. FOLK POP ROCK
00703088 Book/CD Pack.........................$12.99

21. HAWAIIAN CLASSICS
00703097 Book/CD Pack.........................$12.99

23. TAYLOR SWIFT
00704106 Book/CD Pack.........................$14.99

24. WINTER WONDERLAND
00101871 Book/CD Pack.........................$12.99

HAL·LEONARD® CORPORATION

7777 W. BLUEMOUND RD. P.O. BOX 13819 MILWAUKEE, WI 53213

www.halleonard.com

Prices, contents, and availability subject to change without notice.

0313

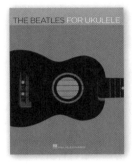

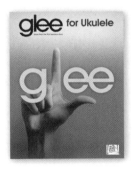

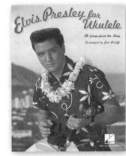

UKULELE CHORD SONGBOOKS

This series features convenient 6" x 9" books with complete lyrics and chord symbols above the lyrics for dozens of great songs. Each song also includes chord grids at the top of every page and the first notes of the melody for easy reference.

ACOUSTIC ROCK

60 tunes: American Pie • Band on the Run • Catch the Wind • Crazy Little Thing Called Love • Daydream • Every Rose Has Its Thorn • Hallelujah • Iris • The Magic Bus • More Than Words • Only Wanna Be with You • Patience • Seven Bridges Road • The Sound of Silence • Space Oddity • Sweet Talkin' Woman • 3 AM • Wake up Little Susie • Who'll Stop the Rain • and more.
00702482 Lyrics/Chord Symbols/
Ukulele Chord Diagrams....................$14.99

THE BEATLES

100 favorites: Across the Universe • Carry That Weight • Dear Prudence • Good Day Sunshine • Here Comes the Sun • If I Fell • Love Me Do • Michelle • Ob-La-Di, Ob-La-Da • Revolution • Something • Ticket to Ride • We Can Work It Out • and many more.
00703065 Lyrics/Chord Symbols/Ukulele
Chord Diagrams......................................$17.99

CHILDREN'S SONGS

80 classics: Alphabet Song • "C" Is for Cookie • Do-Re-Mi • I'm Popeye the Sailor Man • John Jacob Jingleheimer Schmidt • Mickey Mouse March • Oh! Susanna • Polly Wolly Doodle • Puff the Magic Dragon • The Rainbow Connection • Sing • Three Little Fishies (Itty Bitty Poo) • Won't You Be My Neighbor? (It's a Beautiful Day in the Neighborhood) • and many more.
00702473 Lyrics/Chord Symbols/
Ukulele Chord Diagrams...................$14.99

CHRISTMAS CAROLS

75 favorites: Away in a Manger • Coventry Carol • Ding Dong! Merrily on High! • The First Noel • Good King Wenceslas • Hark! the Herald Angels Sing • I Saw Three Ships • Joy to the World • O Little Town of Bethlehem • Rise Up, Shepherd, and Follow • Still, Still, Still • Up on the Housetop • We Wish You a Merry Christmas • What Child Is This? • and more.
00702474 Lyrics/Chord Symbols/
Ukulele Chord Diagrams...................$14.99

ISLAND SONGS

60 beach party tunes: Blue Hawaii • Day-O (The Banana Boat Song) • Don't Worry, Be Happy • Island Girl • It's Five O'Clock Somewhere • Kokomo • Lovely Hula Girl • Mele Kalikimaka • No Woman No Cry • One Paddle, Two Paddle • Red, Red Wine • Surfer Girl • Tiny Bubbles • Ukulele Lady • and many more.
00702471 Lyrics/Chord Symbols/
Ukulele Chord Diagrams....................$16.99

THREE CHORD SONGS

60 songs: All Along the Watchtower • Bad Case of Loving You • Bang a Gong (Get It On) • Blue Suede Shoes • Cecilia • Do Wah Diddy Diddy • Get Back • Hound Dog • Kiss • La Bamba • Me and Bobby McGee • Not Fade Away • Rock This Town • Sweet Home Chicago • Twist and Shout • You Are My Sunshine • and more.
00702483 Lyrics/Chord Symbols/
Ukulele Chord Diagrams....................$14.99

HAL•LEONARD® CORPORATION
7777 W. BLUEMOUND RD. P.O. BOX 13819 MILWAUKEE, WI 53213

www.halleonard.com

0812